# Vocabulary
# in practice 3

*Glennis Pye*

40 units of
self-study
vocabulary
exercises

**with tests**

D1434049

**CAMBRIDGE**
UNIVERSITY PRESS

PUBLISHED BY THE PRESS SYNDICATE OF THE UNIVERSITY OF CAMBRIDGE
The Pitt Building, Trumpington Street, Cambridge, United Kingdom

CAMBRIDGE UNIVERSITY PRESS
The Edinburgh Building, Cambridge CB2 2RU, UK
40 West 20th Street, New York, NY 10011–4211, USA
477 Williamstown Road, Port Melbourne, VIC 3207, Australia
Ruiz de Alarcón 13, 28014 Madrid, Spain
Dock House, The Waterfront, Cape Town 8001, South Africa
http://www.cambridge.org

First published 2003
Reprinted 2003

Printed in Italy by G. Canale & C. S.p.A.

*Typeface* Bembo 10/11pt    *System* QuarkXpress®    [HMCL]

ISBN 0 521 75375 9

# Contents

# To the student

This book will give you the chance to practise your vocabulary in a fun way.

*Vocabulary in Practice 3* has:
- 40 units of short, enjoyable exercises – each unit practises groups of words which belong together
- 4 Tests – one after every 10 units, helping you to remember the words from those units
- an Answer Key
- a Word List – this is a list of all the words in each unit with information about how the words are used.

You can use the book in two ways:
1. Start at the beginning of the book. Do units 1–40 and then do the Tests.
2. Look at the Contents. Do the units you think are important first. When you have finished the book, do the Tests.

You can do each unit in two ways:
1. Do the unit and check your answers in the Answer Key. Study the Word List and learn the words you got wrong. Then do the exercise again.
2. Study the Word List for the unit. Then do the unit and check your answers.

**Note** Do the exercises in this book in pencil. Then you can do the exercises again after a week or a month. Repeating the exercises will help you to remember the words.

Here are some ideas to help you to learn vocabulary:
- Learn groups of words which belong together [e.g. skirt, coat, trousers, etc.].
- Learn a word and also its opposite [e.g. beautiful/ugly, hot/cold].
- Draw pictures: some words are easier to remember if you draw a picture and write the word under it, e.g.

*hand*

*spoon*

*fish*

- Write new words in a notebook: write the meaning in English or in your own language, then write a sentence using the word.

I hope you find this book useful and that it makes learning English words fun.

# 1 The family

**A** Complete what the people are saying with the words in the box.

brother-in-law  daughter-in-law  father-in-law  grandparents
great-grandfather  great-grandmother  mother-in-law  sister-in-law
~~son-in-law~~  step-brother  step-daughter  step-father  step-mother
step-sister  step-son

Bob  Sheila  Faye  Jason  Beth  Simon

Harold  Betty  Rowena  Bernard  Jenny  Paul  Jill  Jack

BERNARD: There's me, next to my daughter, Jenny, and that's Paul, my
(1) ......*son-in-law*...... . That's Paul's (2) .................................. ,
Jack. He and Paul's mother, Jill, got married last year. And there's Paul's
(3) .................................. , Bob and Sheila. They're Jill's parents.

JILL: There's me, next to my son, Paul, and that's Jenny, my
(4) .................................. . That's my other son, Jason, and next
to him are Simon, my (5) .................................. , and Beth, my
(6) .................................. – Jack's children from his first marriage.

JENNY: There's Jill and Jason, my (7) .................................. and
my (8) .................................. . That's Rowena, my
(9) .................................. . She and Dad got married about three years
ago. And there's my (10) .................................. and
(11) .................................. , Betty and Harold – they're my
grandmother's parents. That's my sister, Faye, standing next to Jason.

PAUL: There's Bernard, my (12) .................................. , and Faye, my
(13) .................................. . And that's Beth and Simon, my
(14) .................................. and (15) .................................. .

# 2 People you know

## A Put the words in the box into the correct group.

acquaintance boss boyfriend classmate close friend colleague
friend of the family girlfriend mate neighbour relative

**family**
.................................

**school**
.................................

**where you live**
.................................

**love**
.................................
.................................

**work**
.................................

**other**
..... *acquaintance* ....
.................................
.................................

## B Complete the sentences with one of the words on the right.

1 I have lots of ....... *mates* ......... , but
very few close friends.

classmates / mates

2 He's ......................... , really.
I've only met him a few times.

an acquaintance /
a close friend

3 She's a good ......................... . She
pays me well and is always very fair.

boss / relative

4 I love going to work. My
......................... are great fun.

colleagues / neighbours

5 It's her sixth birthday next week. She's
invited her ......................... to tea.

boyfriends / classmates

6 Do you like your new house? Have
you met your ......................... yet?

friends of the family /
neighbours

7 Our family is quite small, so I
haven't got many ......................... .

girlfriends / relatives

8 Amy's got a new ......................... .

boyfriend / relative

9 Jim isn't my uncle, he's just
a ......................... .

boss / friend of the family

10 Ian says he's going to ask his
......................... to marry him.

colleague / girlfriend

11 If you have a problem, it helps if you
can talk to ......................... about it.

an acquaintance /
a close friend

# 3 Clothes

**A** **Write the clothes words in the box in the correct suitcase.**

bikini  fleece  sandals  sunglasses  sunhat  swimming costume
trunks  walking boots  waterproof jacket

BEACH HOLIDAY

WALKING HOLIDAY

**B** **Label the pictures with the words from A.**

1 ..................    6 ..................    8 ..................
2 ..................    7 ..................    9 ..................
3 ..................
4 ..................
5 ..................

**C** **The underlined words are in the wrong sentences. Write the correct word for each sentence.**

1 You wear <u>underpants</u> on your feet in the house.    *slippers*
2 You wear a <u>bra</u> in the house before you get dressed.  ..................
3 A woman wears <u>slippers</u> under her trousers.  ..................
4 A woman wears a <u>vest</u> in bed.  ..................
5 A man wears <u>pyjamas</u> under his trousers.  ..................
6 A woman wears a <u>dressing gown</u> under her blouse.  ..................
7 A man wears <u>knickers</u> in bed.  ..................
8 You wear a <u>nightie</u> under your jumper.  ..................

# 4 Clothes and accessories

## A Complete the sentences with the words in the box.

belt    bracelet    comb    earrings    ~~lipstick~~
necklace    purse    ring    shoelaces    wallet

**1** One of the women
isn't wearing ....... *lipstick* ....... .

**2** One of the women
isn't wearing .................................. .

**3** One of the dressing tables hasn't
got a .................................. on it.

**4** One of the men hasn't
got a .................................. .

**5** One of the women isn't
wearing a .................................. .

**6** One of the pairs of shoes
hasn't got any .................................. .

**7** One of the women isn't
wearing a .................................. .

**8** One of the dolls isn't
wearing a .................................. .

**9** One of the bags doesn't
have a .................................. .

**10** One of the shops hasn't got
a .................................. .

# 5 Life

## A Look at the pictures and complete the sentences with the words in the box.

| died | fell in love | got divorced | got engaged | got married |
| grew up | had a baby | moved house | retired | started school |
| was born | went to university |

1 Jack ................................................ in the country.

2 When he was two years old, his parents ................................................ .

3 So Jack ................................................ in the city.

4 When he was five years old, Jack ................................................ .

5 At the age of eighteen, he ................................................ .

6 He met Jenny there and ................................................ .

7 They ................................................ immediately.

8 When they finished university, they ................................................ .

9 Soon they ................................................ and were happy for many years.

10 When Jack ................................................ , he and Jenny began to argue.

11 A few years later, they ................................................ .

12 Not long after that, Jack ................................................ .

# 6 Describing character

**A** **Put the words in the box into the correct group.**

generous  impatient  lovely  mean  patient
polite  rude  selfish  sensible  silly

**bad qualities:** ......................................................................................

**good qualities:** ......................................................................................

**B** **Match the sentences on the left with the replies on the right. Write the letters in the box below.**

1 She wants to give me some money as a gift.

2 She just walked straight past without even saying hello.

3 She always says please and thank you.

4 She hates waiting for anything. She wants everything to be done right now.

5 She's very good with the children. I never worry about them when she's there.

6 I really like Rich's new girlfriend.

7 She only thinks about herself.

8 She never gets angry, even when she has to explain things to them again and again.

9 She's always telling jokes and playing tricks on people.

10 He asked if he could use her car to get to the hospital, but she just said no.

a Oh, she's so rude.

b I know, she's very sensible, isn't she?

c I know, she's so selfish, isn't she?

d Yes, she's a very polite girl.

e Yes, she seems lovely, doesn't she?

f I know, she's so impatient, isn't she?

g Oh, she's so mean.

h I think she's too silly sometimes, don't you?

i Yes, she's really patient, isn't she?

j She's always so generous, isn't she?

| 1 ......... | 2 ......... | 3 ......... | 4 ......... | 5 ......... |
| 6 ......... | 7 ......... | 8 ......... | 9 ......... | 10 ......... |

# 7 Describing appearance

**A** Find twelve adjectives for describing appearance in the grid. Then complete the words in the list below.

| d | a | r | k | – | s | k | i | n | n | e | d | p |
|---|---|---|---|---|---|---|---|---|---|---|---|---|
| i | n | c | k | o | l | p | l | o | a | l | w | l |
| n | s | o | n | i | i | g | o | v | n | b | e | a |
| d | c | u | t | e | m | p | r | e | t | t | y | i |
| t | r | e | n | d | y | r | u | r | q | u | e | n |
| r | u | o | c | h | i | n | d | w | h | l | t | x |
| y | f | d | i | n | c | h | o | e | w | p | h | o |
| v | f | a | i | r | – | s | k | i | n | n | e | d |
| o | y | t | z | i | e | l | e | g | a | n | t | o |
| p | j | l | q | u | h | s | g | h | b | e | c | h |
| y | i | a | u | s | m | a | r | t | m | r | a | m |
| t | g | o | o | d | – | l | o | o | k | i | n | g |

1 c _ _ _
2 d _ _ _ - _ _ _ _ _ _ _
3 e _ _ _ _ _ _
4 f _ _ _ - _ _ _ _ _ _ _
5 g _ _ _ - _ _ _ _ _ _ _
6 o _ _ _ _ _ _ _ _ _
7 p _ _ _ _
8 p _ _ _ _ _
9 s _ _ _ _ _ _
10 s _ _ _
11 s _ _ _ _
12 t _ _ _ _ _

**B** Complete what the people are saying with the words from A.

1 Jane's new boyfriend looks like a model. He's very ............................... .

2 If you're going for an interview, you'd better make sure you look ............................... .

3 I'm a bit ............................... . I need to go on a diet.

4 I'm ............................... , so I try to keep out of the sun completely.

5 Oh look! She's so ............................... . How many months old is she?

6 She isn't beautiful, but she isn't ugly either. She's just ............................... .

7 You still have to be careful in the sun even if you're ............................... .

8 He looks really ............................... in his designer clothes.

9 I always look so ............................... . I really need to buy some new clothes.

10 Penny's got a lovely face and beautiful hair. She's very ............................... .

11 I want to be ............................... , but I just don't seem to be able to lose weight.

12 I'm so short. I could never look ............................... .

# 8 How you feel

## A Circle the correct word for each picture.

**1**

(cheerful) / embarrassed

**2**

relaxed / worried

**3**

jealous / pleased

**4**

annoyed / guilty

**5**

miserable / proud

**6**

fed up / surprised

## B Complete the sentences with the other words from A.

**1** I have no job, no money and I can't sleep at night – I feel
so *miserable*.

**2** People think I'm ............................... because she's got a boyfriend and I
haven't.

**3** I feel ............................... about not visiting my grandmother in hospital.

**4** I'm not ............................... they're getting married – they've known each
other a long time.

**5** I'm ............................... about you walking home on your own at night.

**6** And then I just started to cry in front of everyone – I felt
so ............................... .

# 9 Having a bad day

**A** Match the words and expressions on the left with the definitions on the right. Write the letters in the box below.

| | | | |
|---|---|---|---|
| **1** run out of | | **a** | fall to the ground |
| **2** oversleep | | **b** | be in a line of cars that is not moving |
| **3** have an argument | | **c** | not get up early enough |
| **4** break down | | **d** | arrive too late to get on a vehicle |
| **5** fall over | | **e** | not be able to find your way |
| **6** miss | | **f** | stop working |
| **7** get lost | | **g** | make liquid pour somewhere by mistake |
| **8** be late | | **h** | not have any of something left |
| **9** be stuck in a traffic jam | | **i** | arrive after the correct time |
| **10** spill | | **j** | talk angrily with someone |

| **1** | **2** | **3** | **4** | **5** |
|---|---|---|---|---|
| **6** | **7** | **8** | **9** | **10** |

**B** Complete the paragraph with the expressions from A. Remember to write the verbs in the past tense.

I had a very bad day yesterday. I usually get up at seven o'clock, but I
(1) _overslept_ and didn't get up until eight. Then I (2) ............................ the
bus and had to wait twenty minutes for the next one to come. Of course I
(3) ............................ for work and I could see my boss wasn't very pleased.
The rest of the morning was OK, but as I was walking to the staff
restaurant for lunch, I (4) ............................ and hurt my wrist. I was really
happy when it was time to go home. But things didn't get any better,
I'm afraid. There was a new driver on the bus. He went the wrong way and
(5) ............................ . He turned into a very busy road and we
(6) ............................ for about twenty minutes. Then the bus
(7) ............................ petrol and (8) ............................ . I had to get
off and walk the rest of the way home. When I got home, I decided to relax
with a nice cup of tea, but I (9) ............................ it all over my new skirt. I
phoned my boyfriend, thinking he would make me feel better, but
he said something unkind about one of my friends and we
(10) ............................ . I hope today is going to be better.

# 10 Accidents and injuries

**A** **Complete the sentences on the left with the words in the box. Then match the sentences on the left with the reasons on the right. Write the letters in the box below.**

| black broken bruise burn cut ~~swollen~~ |
|---|

1 I've got a ......*swollen*...... ankle.

2 I've got a ..................on my finger.

3 I've got a .................. leg.

4 I've got a nasty .................. on my foot.

5 I've got a .................. eye.

6 I've got an enormous .................. on my forehead.

**a** I got into a fight.

**b** I fell off my motorbike.

**c** I touched a hot iron.

**d** I slipped while I was out running.

**e** I walked into a door.

**f** I stood on some broken glass.

| 1 *d* | 2 | 3 | 4 | 5 | 6 |
|---|---|---|---|---|---|

**B** **Complete the dialogue with the words in the box.**

| bandage  bleeding  had an accident  hurt  injured  pain  stitches  treatment  unconscious |
|---|

Amy: Did you hear? Marcia's (1) .................. . She fell off her bike and landed on her head. She was (2) .................. for about ten minutes. When she woke up, she didn't know where she was.

Kate: Was she badly (3) .................. ?

Amy: Well, her head was (4) .................. and she was in a lot of (5) .................. .

Kate: What (6) .................. did she need?

Amy: She needed a few (7) .................. in her head – she said having them put in (8) .................. more than anything. She's also got a (9) .................. around her wrist.

# Test 1 (Units 1–10)

**A** **Complete the sentences with words for the people in your family and people you know.**

1 This is my .................................... , Ben. My husband's brother.

2 This is my .................................... , Jackie. We sit next to each other at work.

3 This is my .................................... , Hugh. He lives next door.

4 This is my .................................... , Angela. My wife's mother.

5 This is my .................................... , Kath. My dad's new wife.

6 This is my .................................... . My mum's granddad.

7 This is my .................................... , David. I've worked for him for three years.

8 This is my .................................... , Max. He's my husband's son from his first marriage.

**B** **Match the words in the box with Gemma and Sarah's appearance. Then write lists of what the girls are wearing.**

| overweight   plain   pretty   scruffy   slim   smart |

**Gemma**          **appearance**          **Sarah**

......................          ......................

......................          ......................

......................          ......................

**clothes and accessories**

......................          ......................

......................          ......................

......................          ......................

......................          ......................

......................

......................

**C** When do we usually do these things in our life? Put the
words in the box in the correct order.

> be born   die   fall in love   get engaged   get married
> have a baby   retire   start school

1 .................... 2 .................... 3 .................... 4 ....................
5 .................... 6 .................... 7 .................... 8 ....................

**D** What are the people like? Match the words in the box with
what they are saying.

> generous   impatient   selfish   sensible   silly   rude

1 Have my chocolate – I can get some more. ....................
2 I don't care about them – I've got my own problems. ....................
3 Let's put jam all around his mouth while he's asleep! ....................
4 Come on, hurry up! I can't wait any longer! ....................
5 Move! That's my chair. ....................
6 Let's cross the road at the zebra crossing. It's safer there. ....................

**E** Complete the sentences with one word or expression from
each box. Remember to put the verbs in the correct form.

> annoyed   embarrassed
> guilty   miserable
> pleased   worried

> be late   fall over   have an accident
> have an argument   not be in pain   spill

1 She's .................... because she .................... with her
boyfriend last night.
2 She's .................... because she .................... in front
of the whole class.
3 She's .................... because he .................... coffee all
over her carpet.
4 She feels .................... because she hasn't visited a friend who
.................... last week.
5 She's .................... because he .................... and she
thinks they're going to miss their train.
6 She's .................... because the drugs worked and she
.................... any more.

17

# 11 Shops and shopping

## A Label the pictures with the words in the box.

baker's    basket    butcher's    checkout    chemist's    clothes shop    trolley
department store    gift shop    hairdresser's    newsagent's    supermarket

1 ................................    2 ................................    3 ................................    4 ................................

5 ................................    6 ................................    7 ................................    8 ................................

9 ................................    10 ................................    11 ................................    12 ................................

## B Complete the paragraph with the words in the box.

changing room    cost    fit    pay    receipt    shop assistant    till    try on

At the weekend I went shopping for a new pair of jeans. There were
so many different types, I didn't know which ones to choose. A
(1) ................................................ came over and asked me if I needed any
help. 'Why don't you (2) ................................ a few pairs?' she suggested.

'Good idea,' I replied. 'Then I can see if they (3) ................................ me.'

'There's a (4) ................................................ just over there,' she said.

After deciding which pair I liked best, I checked the label to see how
much they (5) ................................ . They were quite cheap so I decided to buy
two pairs. I took them to the man at the (6) ................................ .

'Can I (7) ................................ by cheque or credit card?' I asked.

'Yes, of course,' he replied. 'Would you like me to put your
(8) ................................ in the bag? You should keep it in case you want to bring
them back.'

# 12 Houses and homes

## A Match the people with their homes.

I live in a bungalow. ☐

I live in a house. [1]

I live in a flat. ☐

I live in a cottage. ☐

## B Label the pictures with the words in the box.

| block of   detached   semi-detached   terraced |

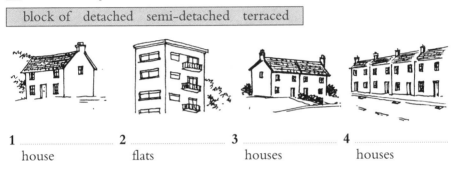

1 .................... 2 .................... 3 .................... 4 ....................

house      flats      houses      houses

## C Look at the picture and complete the sentences with the words in the box.

| basement   first floor   ground floor   second floor |

1 Jamie is spending £95,000.
   He's buying the .................... flat.

2 Laura is spending £85,000.
   She's buying the .................... flat.

3 Helena is spending £110,000.
   She's buying the .................... flat.

4 Marc is spending £70,000.
   He's buying the .................... flat.

FOR SALE
£85,000

FOR SALE
£110,000

FOR SALE
£95,000

FOR SALE
£70,000

# 13 Housework

## A  Label the pictures with the words in the box.

> dishwasher   dustbin   duster   iron   ironing board   pegs
> vacuum cleaner   washing line   washing machine

1 .................................................
2 .................................................
3 .................................................
4 .................................................
5 .................................................
6 .................................................
7 .................................................
8 .................................................
9 .................................................

## B  What do you use when you need to do these jobs around the house? Put the words from A into the correct group.

do the dishes

.................................................

do the ironing

.................................................
.................................................

do the washing

.................................................
.................................................
.................................................

dust

.................................................

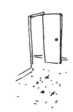

hoover

.................................................

put the rubbish out

.................................................

# 14 In the kitchen

## A Label the pictures with the words in the box.

bottle opener   coffee maker   corkscrew   food processor   frying pan
mug   pan   tap   teapot   tea towel   tin opener   washing-up liquid

1 ............................   2 ............................   3 ............................

4 ............................   5 ............................   6 ............................

7 ............................   8 ............................   9 ............................

10 ............................   11 ............................   12 ............................

## B Put the words from A into the correct group.

| for cleaning | for opening things | for drinks | for cooking |
|---|---|---|---|
| .................... | .................... | .................... | .................... |
| .................... | .................... | .................... | .................... |
| .................... | .................... | .................... | .................... |

# 15 Food

## A Tick the eight items Gary has already put in the shopping trolley.

aubergine .................
bacon .................
bread rolls ✓.............
cereal .................
cheese .................
cucumber .................
dried fruit .............
eggs .................
frozen vegetables .............
melon .................
red pepper .............
pineapple .............
sausages .............
tinned fruit .................

## B Label the pictures with the other words from A.

1 .................

2 .................

3 .................

4 .................

5 .................

6 .................

# 16 Health and fitness

## A Match the words in the box with the definitions.

be bad for you   be good for you   ~~exercise~~   fit   ~~healthy~~   healthy diet
keep fit   lose weight   put on weight   unfit   unhealthy

1 physically strong and not likely to get ill ............... *healthy* ...............
2 physically strong because you do enough exercise ...............
3 to become thinner ...............
4 to be good for your health ...............
5 physical activity that you do to make your body strong and healthy ...............
6 to stay healthy ...............
7 to be likely to damage your health ...............
8 not physically strong because you do not do enough exercise ...............
9 food that is good for your health ...............
10 to become fatter ...............
11 to not be good for your health ...............

## B Complete the paragraph with the words from A. Remember to put the verbs in the correct form.

### Health and fitness

Do you feel good? Are you (1) *fit* and (2) ............................... ?
Maybe you think you are too fat and need to (3) ............................... .
Or maybe you are too thin and need to (4) ............................... . Here is
some advice for you. First of all, it is important not to do things that are
(5) ............................... – so, give up smoking or try to smoke less,
do not drink too much alcohol or go to bed too late. If you have an
(6) ............................... lifestyle, try to change some of the things
you do – do things that are (7) ............................... . Make sure you eat a
(8) ............................... , including plenty of fresh fruit and vegetables.
Do plenty of (9) ............................... to (10) ............................... – go
running or join your local gym. If you are very (11) ............................... ,
though, you should start with just a little swimming.

# 17 Sport

**A** **Where do you do these sports? Match the sports with the places.**

court ☐

track ☐

pitch ☐

**B** **Complete the paragraphs about the sports in A with the words in the box. You can use some of the words more than once. Remember to put the verbs in the correct form.**

| game goal lose match player point race score team win |
| --- |

He's practising for tomorrow's football (1) .............................. .
He's a very good (2) .............................. . He hopes he'll
(3) .............................. a (4) .............................. and help his
(5) .............................. to (6) .............................. . He won't be happy
if they (7) .............................. .

She's playing a (8) .............................. of tennis. She's just
(9) .............................. a (10) .............................. and needs only one
more to (11) .............................. . She's quite a good tennis
(12) .............................. .

He's running so fast – I think he's going to (13) .............................. the
(14) .............................. .

# 18 Music

## A Put the words in the box into the correct group.

band   choir   classical music   composer   conductor   jazz
opera   orchestra   pop music   pop star   singer

**types of music**                    **people**

............................          ............................          ............................

............................          ............................          ............................

............................          ............................          ............................

............................          ............................

## B Match the people with the type of music they like.

1        2        3        4

I like opera.                    ☐

I like classical music.          ☐

I like jazz.                     ☐

I like pop music.                ☐

## C Complete what the people are saying with the words for people from A.

JONATHAN: Last night I saw the opera Don Giovanni. The
(1) ............................ who was Don Giovanni had a fantastic voice.
The music was wonderful too, and the (2) ............................
controlled the (3) ............................ very well.

BEN: I love classical music and I sing in a small (4) ............................ .
Next week we're giving a concert of 18th century music by the
(5) ............................ Mozart.

CHARLOTTE: My young cousin loves pop music. She's a member of a
(6) ............................ and wants to become a famous
(7) ............................ .

# 19 Shapes

**A** Look at the picture. Then complete the answers with the words in the box. Remember to use the plural form if you need to.

> circle   diamond   heart   oval
> rectangle   square   star   triangle

1  What shape is the car?                          It's a ........... *star* ...........
2  What shape is the clock face?                   It's a ................................. .
3  What shape is the door of the house?            It's a ................................. .
4  What shape are the windows of the house?        They're ............................. .
5  What shape is the sun?                          It's a ................................. .
6  What shape are the wheels on the bicycle?       They're ............................. .
7  What shape is the cat's body?                   It's a ................................. .
8  What shape are the windows of the church?       They're ............................. .
9  What shape is the chimney on the house?         It's a ................................. .
10  What shape are the cat's ears?                 They're ............................. .
11  What shape is the roof of the house?           It's a ................................. .
12  What shape are the wheels on the car?          They're ............................. .

**B** Complete the sentences about the picture in A with the words in the box.

> circular   diamond-shaped   heart-shaped   oval
> rectangular   square   star-shaped   triangular

1  It's a ........................... house with four ........................... windows,
   a ........................... door and a ........................... roof.
2  It's a ........................... car with ........................... wheels.
3  It's a bike with ........................... wheels.
4  It's a cat with an ........................... body and ........................... ears.
5  It's a church with ........................... windows.

# 20 Measurements

**A** **Complete the measurements with the words in the box.**

depth   height   length   weight   width

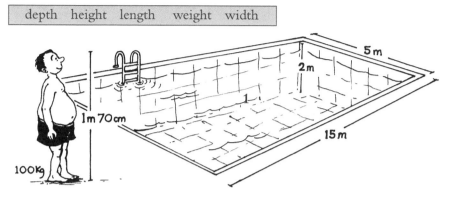

**swimming pool**

1 .................................. 15m
2 .................................. 5m
3 .................................. 2m

**man**

1 .................................. 1m 70cm
2 .................................. 100kg

**B** **Complete the questions about the items below with the words in the box.**

deep   heavy   high   long   tall   weigh   wide

1 How .................................. is it?
2 How .................................. is it?
3 How .................................. is it?
4 How .................................. is it?

5 How .................................. is she?
6 How .................................. is it?
7 How much does he .................................. ?

# Test 2 (Units 11–20)

## A Complete the sentences with words for shops or houses.

1 I need to buy a newspaper. Is there a _____ around here?

2 I need something for my headache. Where is the _____ ?

3 Where I live, there is another house on each side. I live in a _____ house.

4 I live in a house in the countryside. I live in a _____ .

## B Complete the sentences with words for types of housework.

1 The vacuum cleaner has broken, so I can't _____ .

2 The dishwasher has broken, so I can't do the _____ .

3 The iron has broken, so I can't do the _____ .

4 I haven't got a duster, so I can't _____ .

## C The underlined words are in the wrong sentences. Write the correct word for each sentence.

1 Can you dry the cups for me? The teapot is over there. ..........................

2 I'll open this bottle of wine. Could you pass me the tin opener? ..........................

3 To make fried eggs, first get the tea towel really hot. ..........................

4 Have a beer. Here's the frying pan. ..........................

5 It's a small corkscrew, so you can only make two cups of tea. ..........................

6 I need a bottle opener to open this tin. ..........................

## D Find the first letter and write the words for the foods.

1 small round objects we get from a chicken
..........................

2 meat from a pig cut into thin slices
..........................

3 solid food made from milk
..........................

4 meat pressed into a long tube shape
..........................

## E Complete what the people are saying.

1 I'm so ............................. . I really don't do enough exercise.

2 Let's have a ............................. – to see who can run the fastest.

3 I like to eat ............................. food – lots of fresh fruit and vegetables.

4 They were lucky. They ............................. a goal in the last minute.

## F Follow the lines. Then complete the sentences.

1 He's in a ............................. band.

2 He's a member of an ............................. .

3 He's a member of a ............................. .

4 He's a ............................. .

## G Follow the instructions and draw the shapes.

Draw a big circle. In the middle of the circle draw a small triangle. Under the triangle draw a rectangle. Above the triangle draw two small ovals. Inside each oval draw a diamond.

## H Complete the sentences with words for measurement.

1 What's the ............................. of this piece of wood?     It's 3m long.

2 How ............................. is this box?     It weighs 3.5kg.

3 What's the ............................. of this room?     It's 3m wide.

4 How ............................. are you?     I'm 1m 67cm.

# 21 Jobs

**A** Look at the table and complete the answers with the words in the box.

|  | things done in job | hours worked |
|---|---|---|
| **Janice** | dusts, hoovers, irons, etc. | 3 afternoons/week |
| **Eric** | takes photos | 5 days/week |
| **Lena** | keeps records of money for a company | 3 days/week |
| **Tim** | works for the government | 5 days/week |
| **Michelle** | writes instructions for computers | 5 days/week |

> an accountant   a civil servant   a cleaner
> a computer programmer   a photographer

1  What does Janice do?     She's _____ .
2  What does Eric do?     He's _____ .
3  What does Lena do?     She's _____ .
4  What does Tim do?     He's _____ .
5  What does Michelle do?     She's _____ .

**B** Look at the table in A again. Complete the sentences with the names of the people from A.

1  _____Eric_____ , _____ and _____ work full-time.
2  _____ and _____ work part-time.

**C** Complete the advertisements with the words in the box.

> au pair   journalist   model   shop assistant

1
**WANTED** _____
to write news stories for
local newspaper.

2
**WANTED** _____
to work at the London Fashion Show.
Must be tall, thin and beautiful.

3
**WANTED** _____
to look after two children
aged 5 and 8. Must speak
good English.

4  **WANTED** _____
to sell clothing in busy department
store. Must be smart and polite.

# 22 In the office

**A** Label the picture with the words in the box.

> calculator   desk tidy   diary   file   filing cabinet
> hole punch   in-tray/out-tray   notepad   paper clip
> Post-it™ note   ring binder   stapler

1 ........................................
2 ........................................
3 ........................................
4 ........................................
5 ........................................
6 ........................................
7 ........................................
8 ........................................
9 ........................................
10 ........................................
11 ........................................
12 ........................................

**B** Complete the sentences with words from A.

1 Have you got a ........................................ ? I need to fasten these pages together, but I don't want to make a hole in them.

2 Have you got a ........................................ ? I want to fasten these pages together.

3 There are pens, pencils, rubbers and all sorts of things all over my desk. I need a ........................................ .

4 Don't worry, I won't forget. I'll write 'meet Sandy at 2 o'clock' on a ........................................ and stick it on my computer.

5 Take a ........................................ to the meeting so that you can write down the things you need to remember.

6 I have this ........................................ to write down the days and times I have to do things.

# 23 Writing to people

**A** The <u>underlined</u> words are in the wrong sentences. Write the correct word for each sentence.

1 The boss sent us <u>a fax</u>, reminding us that we should dress smartly for work.

2 Paul wrote Jenny <u>a postcard</u> explaining why he didn't want to see her any more.

3 We're going on holiday next week – we'll send you <u>a memo</u>.

4 Use your computer and send him <u>a note</u> – it's the quickest way of contacting someone.

5 Mum left me <u>an email</u> asking me to buy milk and bread.

6 Can you send <u>a text message</u>? That'll be quick and we'll have a copy of your order.

7 I've got a mobile phone, but I don't know how to send <u>a letter</u> on it.

**B** Label the picture with the words in the box.

address   envelope   postcode   stamp   writing paper

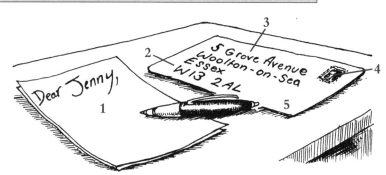

1 ....................................

2 ....................................

3 ....................................

4 ....................................

5 ....................................

# 24 Holidays

**A  Complete the sentences with the words in the box.**

beach holiday  camping holiday  cruise  skiing holiday  walking holiday

1  I love sleeping outside. I'm going on a ........................................ .

2  I love lying in the sun. I'm going on a ........................................ .

3  I love the mountains in the summer. I'm going on a ........................................ .

4  I love the mountains in the winter. I'm going on a ........................................ .

5  I love the sea. I'm going on a ........................................ .

**B  Complete the sentences with the words in the box.**

bed and breakfast  hotels  tent  villas  youth hostel

**PANNE ISLAND.** *Where to stay.*
If you like to be comfortable in a place where everything is done for you,
there are several excellent (1)........................................ to choose from. If you
cannot afford one of these, the (2) ........................................ is very cheap and
a good place to meet other young people. If you like to cook for yourself,
there are many attractive (3) ........................................ , some with their own
swimming pool. If all you want is somewhere to sleep and eat breakfast,
you could try a (4) ........................................ . Finally, if you have a
(5) ........................................ , there are several very good campsites in the south.

**C  Match the things you should do on the left with the reasons on the right. Write the letters in the box below.**

Before you go on holiday abroad you should:

1  buy some foreign currency          **a**  to find out more about the
                                          country you are going to

2  buy a guidebook                    **b**  to stop you from getting diseases
3  have vaccinations if you need them  **c**  so that you can get into the
                                          country you are going to

4  get a visa if you need it          **d**  so that you can buy things

1 ............  2 ............  3 ............  4 ............

# 25 Hotels

## A Match the words on the left with the definitions on the right. Write the letters in the box below.

1 room service
2 half board
3 receptionist
4 full board
5 reception
6 double room
7 single room
8 twin room
9 book
10 fully booked
11 ensuite
12 reservation

a a room in a hotel with two beds
b a person in a hotel who deals with guests when they arrive
c when you have food or drink brought to your room in a hotel
d having a bathroom attached
e when you pay only to have a room, your breakfast and dinner in a hotel
f an arrangement to have a room in a hotel
g make an arrangement to have a room in a hotel
h when you pay to have a room and all your meals in a hotel
i a room in a hotel with one bed for two people
j the place you go to in a hotel when you arrive
k when all the rooms in a hotel are being used
l a room in a hotel with one bed for one person

| 1 | 2 | 3 | 4 | 5 | 6 |
|---|---|---|---|---|---|
| 7 | 8 | 9 | 10 | 11 | 12 |

## B Complete the phone conversation with words from A.

Receptionist: Hello, The Wiseman Arms Hotel. How can I help you?

Customer: Hello, I'd like to make a (1) .............................. , please. I'd like to (2) .............................. a room for two for the night of 6th October.

Receptionist: I'm sorry, but we're (3) .............................. that night.

Customer: What about the night of 27th October?

Receptionist: Yes, that would be fine. Would you like a double room or a (4) .............................. ?

Customer: A double room, please.

Receptionist: We have a double room with an (5) .............................. bathroom.

Customer: That would be fine. Thank you.

# 26 Travelling by plane

**A** Complete the sentences with the words in the box.

> arrivals   baggage reclaim   check–in desk   customs
> departure lounge   departures   gate   passport control

1 You go to .................................. when you are going somewhere by plane.
2 You say that you have arrived for your flight at the .................................. .
3 You show your passport at .................................. when you are leaving or coming into a country.
4 You wait in the .................................. until it is time to get on your plane.
5 You get on or off a plane at the .................................. .
6 You go to .................................. to get back your bags after your flight.
7 Your bags are checked for illegal goods when you are going into a country at .................................. .
8 You meet someone who is arriving after a flight at .................................. .

**B** Complete what the flight attendant is saying with the words in the box.

> aboard   boarding card   flight   hand luggage
> landing   life jacket   overhead locker   take-off

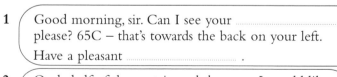

1 Good morning, sir. Can I see your .................................. , please? 65C – that's towards the back on your left. Have a pleasant .................................. .

2 On behalf of the captain and the crew, I would like to welcome you .................................. .

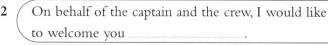

3 Please put all .................................. in the .................................. .

4 There is a .................................. under your seat for use in an emergency.

5 Please remain seated during .................................. and .................................. .

# 27 In the countryside

**A** Look at the picture and complete the sentences with the words in the box.

> bridge farm fields ~~footpath~~ forest lake lane mountains river valley village waterfall

Take the (1) *footpath* until you get to the (2) ........................... .
Walk across the (3) ........................... and then follow the
(4) ........................... . Go across the small (5) ........................... .
Turn right when you see the (6) ........................... . You will see a
(7) ........................... in front of you. Walk through it and you will come
to a small (8) ........................... . In the distance, you will be able to see
the (9) ........................... and the (10) ........................... between them.
Walk to the other side of the lake and then go down the
(11) ........................... , which will take you to the (12) ........................... .

# 28 The weather

**A** Complete the sentences with the words in the boxes. Use the words in the left-hand box more than once.

| east    north |
|---------------|
| south    west |

| forecast   frost ❋   hail ⟳   icy ⌀   sunshine ☼ |
|--------------------------------------------------|
| mild 🌡   showers ☁   thunder and lightning ⚡ |

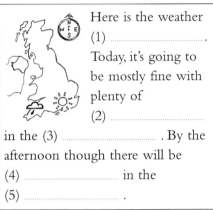

Here is the weather (1) .................... .
Today, it's going to be mostly fine with plenty of (2) ....................
in the (3) .................... . By the afternoon though there will be (4) .................... in the (5) .................... .

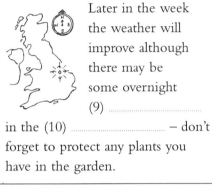

Later in the week the weather will improve although there may be some overnight (9) ....................
in the (10) .................... – don't forget to protect any plants you have in the garden.

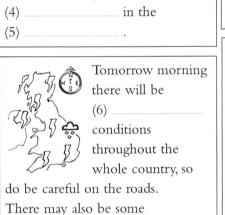

Tomorrow morning there will be (6) ....................
conditions throughout the whole country, so do be careful on the roads.
There may also be some (7) .................... in the (8) .................... .

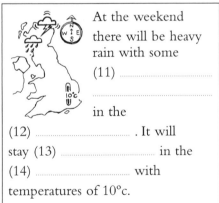

At the weekend there will be heavy rain with some (11) ....................
.................... in the (12) .................... . It will stay (13) .................... in the (14) .................... with temperatures of 10°c.

# 29 Animals

**A** **Put the words in the box into the correct group.**

> bear   butterfly   crab   deer   fly   fox   frog   kangaroo
> octopus   owl   rat   shark   spider   whale

| animals with wings | animals that live in water | other |
|---|---|---|
| ................................ | ................................ | ................................ |
| ................................ | ................................ | ................................ |
| ................................ | ................................ | ................................ |
| | ................................ | ................................ |
| | ................................ | ................................ |
| | | ................................ |

**B** **Label the animals with words from A.**

1 ........................   2 ........................   3 ........................   4 ........................

5 ........................   6 ........................   7 ........................

**C** **Complete the sentences with the other words from A.**

1 An ........................ stays awake at night.
2 A ........................ moves around by jumping. It lives in Australia.
3 A ........................ has eight legs and doesn't live in water.
4 A ........................ walks sideways.
5 An ........................ has eight legs.
6 A ........................ has very sharp teeth.
7 A ........................ has a beautiful pattern on its wings.

# 30 Parts of a car

## A Label the picture with the words in the box.

> boot   bumper   engine   headlight   indicator   seatbelt   tyre
> wheel   windscreen   windscreen wipers   wing mirror

1 ................................
2 ................................
3 ................................
4 ................................
5 ................................
6 ................................
7 ................................
8 ................................
9 ................................
10 ................................
11 ................................

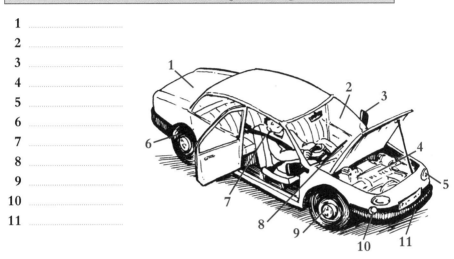

## B Complete the sentences with words from A. Remember to use the plural form if you need to.

1 If it's dark, remember to switch on the ................................ .

2 Before any journey, check that the ................................ have enough air in them.

3 It's a large car with room for lots of luggage in the ................................ .

4 Use the right ................................ to tell other drivers you are turning right.

5 Always fasten your ................................ before starting to drive.

6 If it's raining, turn on the ................................ .

# Test 3 (Units 21–30)

**A** **Complete the sentences with words for jobs.**

1 I write for a local newspaper. I'm a ............................... .

2 I work for the government. I'm a ............................... .

3 I sell clothes in a department store. I'm a ............................... .

4 I keep records of money for a company. I'm an ............................... .

**B** **Complete the sentences.**

1 You use a ............................... to hold several pieces of paper together.

2 You use a ............................... to do mathematical calculations.

3 You put all your pens and pencils in a ............................... .

4 You should keep all your files in a ............................... .

**C** **Label the picture.**

1 ...............................

2 ...............................

3 ...............................

4 ...............................

5 ...............................

**D** **Complete the sentences.**

1 If you've got a fax machine, you could send me a ............................... .

2 If you've got a computer and a modem, you could send me an ............................... .

3 If you've got a mobile phone, you could send me a ............................... .

4 If you've got a pen, some writing paper and an envelope, you could send me a ............................... .

**E** **Complete the paragraphs with words for holidays, hotels and travelling by plane.**

Last year I decided to go on a (1) .............................. . I wanted to lie in the sun and swim in the sea for a change. I went on my own, so I called a hotel and (2) .............................. a (3) .............................. room. My (4) ..............................was very early in the morning. While I was waiting in the (5) .............................. after checking in, I bought myself a (6) .............................. so that I could read about the area I was going to. I put it in my (7) .............................. so that I could look at it on the plane. Actually, I finished reading it before (8) .............................. – we had to wait two hours before we could leave because the pilot was ill.

**F** **Look at the picture and complete the sentences with words for the weather.**

1 There will be .............................. in the west.
2 There will be .............................. in the north.
3 There will be .............................. in the south.
4 There will be .............................. in the east.

**G** **Put the letters in order. Then put the animals into the correct group.**

| brac    krash    lewah    lfy    reutbylft    wlo |

**animals that can fly**                    **animals that can swim**

.............................                .............................

.............................                .............................

.............................                .............................

**H** **Complete the sentences about cars.**

1 Can you see through the .............................. ? It's really dirty.
2 Put that really big bag in the .............................. .
3 Never drive without fastening your .............................. .
4 What's wrong with the .............................. ? The car's making a strange noise.

# 31 Everyday adjectives

**A** Join the words with the opposite meanings.

1 smooth      light
2 sharp      dry
3 light      bent
4 heavy      rough
5 straight      dark
6 wet      blunt

**B** Label the pictures with the words from A.

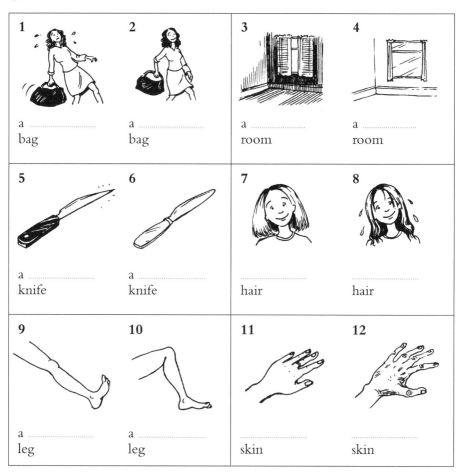

| 1 a ...................... bag | 2 a ...................... bag | 3 a ...................... room | 4 a ...................... room |
| 5 a ...................... knife | 6 a ...................... knife | 7 ...................... hair | 8 ...................... hair |
| 9 a ...................... leg | 10 a ...................... leg | 11 ...................... skin | 12 ...................... skin |

# 32 Using your voice

## A Circle the correct verb and complete the sentence by writing it in the correct form.

1 'Shh, the baby's asleep,' she ............................ .          laugh / whisper

2 Do you ............................ Japanese?          speak / stutter

3 Can you two girls please stop ............................ !          cheer / talk

4 What did you ............................ at the concert?          shout / sing

5 Don't ............................ . Mummy'll be          chat / cry
back soon.

6 'We're getting married,' he ............................ .          announce / tell

7 'I want to go to bed,' he ............................ in a          say / scream
tired voice.

## B Complete the crossword with the other words from A.

1 repeat the first part of a word several times because you have a speech problem
2 talk to someone in a friendly and informal way
3 say something very loudly
4 say something to someone, usually giving them information
5 make the sound of being happy or amused
6 cry or say something loudly, usually because you are afraid or angry
7 give a loud shout of encouragement

# 33 Using your hands

**A** Label the pictures with the words in the box.

clap   knock   pat   pick   pinch   point   scratch   stroke   tickle   wave

1 ......................
2 ......................
3 ......................
4 ......................
5 ......................
6 ......................
7 ......................
8 ......................
9 ......................
10 ......................

**B** Use the expressions in the box and write sentences to describe the pictures in A.

her arm   the little boy   the cat   on the door   his head
the dog's head   a flower   ~~to his friend~~   to a word
because they enjoyed the show

1 *He's waving to his friend.* ......................
2 ......................
3 ......................
4 ......................
5 ......................
6 ......................
7 ......................
8 ......................
9 ......................
10 ......................

# 34 Do and *make*

## A Put the words in the box into the correct group.

business   a cake   exercise   friends   your homework
the housework   a mistake   money   a noise   your teeth

**do**

...... *business* ........

...............................

...............................

...............................

...............................

**make**

...............................

...............................

...............................

...............................

...............................

## B Match the words in the box with the pictures. Complete the phrases with *do* and *make*.

an appointment   the bed   a cup of tea   the dishes   an exam
your hair   lunch   a phone call   the shopping   a speech

1 ...... *make a speech* ......
2 ...............................
3 ...............................
4 ...............................
5 ...............................

6 ...............................
7 ...............................
8 ...............................
9 ...............................
10 ...............................

# 35 Irregular past tenses

**A** **Put the letters in order to find the past tense of the verbs in the list.**

| roftog dunof tsol guatht melts ~~tib~~ webl |
| oder tpu petk rewd boker hrtwe werg |

1 bite    *bit*

8 keep   ................

2 blow   ................

9 lose   ................

3 break   ................

10 put   ................

4 draw   ................

11 ride   ................

5 find   ................

12 smell   ................

6 forget   ................

13 teach   ................

7 grow   ................

14 throw   ................

**B** **Complete the sentences with the verbs in the past tense from A.**

1 No one had been in the house for years and it ................ horrible.

2 He ................ the ball to her.

3 I ................ my wallet while I was out shopping the other day.

4 We ................ our bikes all the way to the beach.

5 He ................ the flowers in some water.

6 He was going to stroke the dog, but it ................ him on the leg.

7 She ................ on her tea before drinking it.

8 We looked everywhere for the key, but we never ................ it.

9 I ................ to send him a birthday card.

10 I ................ the photos for a long time before throwing them out.

11 All the children ................ pictures of themselves.

12 Who ................ my glasses? Fixing them will be very expensive.

13 She ................ English in Japan for three years.

14 She ................ about 2cm last year.

# 36 Phrasal verbs with *off* and *up*

**A** Complete the phrasal verbs with *off* or *up*.

1 I've tried to give .................... smoking, but it's very difficult.
2 Put the milk in the fridge, so it doesn't go .................... .
3 The plane took .................... 30 minutes late.
4 I was brought .................... by my grandparents.
5 My mum's always telling me .................... for putting my feet on the chairs.
6 I'm saving .................... to buy myself a DVD player.
7 When I grow .................... , I'd like to be a doctor.
8 Nobody likes him – he's always showing .................... .
9 You really should phone her. Why do you keep putting it .................... ?
10 If you don't hurry .................... , we're going to be late.

**B** Label the pictures with phrasal verbs from A.

1  *grow up*  2  ....................  3  ....................

4  ....................  5  ....................  6  ....................

**C** Match the other phrasal verbs from A with the definitions.

1 look after and teach a child until they are old enough to look after themselves  *bring up*
2 something you say to someone when you want them to do something quickly  ....................
3 stop doing something that you usually do  ....................
4 become too old and bad to eat  ....................

# 37 More phrasal verbs

**A** Complete the sentences with the verbs in the box. Use each verb twice and remember to put the verb in the correct form.

| fill get look run take |

1 Were you frightened? Why did you ........_run_........ away?
2 He had flu and it took him a long time to ........................... over it.
3 If you want a credit card, you'll have to ........................... in this form.
4 ........................... out! There's a car coming.
5 Do you ........................... on with your boyfriend's family?
6 They were ........................... over by a bigger company last year.
7 Who ........................... after the children when you're at work?
8 We've ........................... out of milk – do you mind black coffee?
9 I went round the room ........................... up everyone's glass.
10 In character, do you ........................... after your mum or your dad?

**B** Label the pictures with phrasal verbs from A.

1 ........................... 2 ........................... 3 ........................... 4 ...........................

**C** Match the other phrasal verbs from A with the definitions.

1 take care of someone ...........................
2 be similar to an older member of your family ...........................
3 write information on an official document ...........................
4 have a good relationship with someone ...........................
5 feel better after being ill ...........................
6 take control of something ...........................

# 38 Sorry and thank you

**A** Complete the sentences with the words in the box.

apologise   matter   mention   mind   ~~OK~~   problem
sorry   thank   thanks   welcome   worry

1 You'll have to wait another 15 minutes.

That's ...... *OK* ...... . I'm not in a hurry.

2 Thanks for telling me about this.

No ...................... . I thought you should know about it.

3 We're so late. We've missed the train now, haven't we?

Yes, but it doesn't ...................... . We can catch the next one.

4 It was really very kind of you to give me a lift home.

Oh, don't ...................... it. I was coming past your house anyway.

5 I upset him because I said I thought his hair looked terrible.

That wasn't very nice. I think you should ...................... .

6 I've done the dishes and tidied the living room for you.

Oh, ...................... you for doing all that. You really didn't have to.

7 I'm afraid we won't be able to come on Saturday night.

Oh well, never ...................... . We'll see you on Sunday anyway.

8 It's so untidy in here.

I'm ...................... . I haven't had time to tidy up yet.

9 Oops! I've spilt some of my drink.

Don't ...................... . It'll clean off easily.

10 Have another drink.

Oh, ...................... .

11 Thank you so much for the lovely flowers.

You're ...................... .

# 39 Giving directions

## A Complete the dialogue with the phrases in the box.

> car park   could you tell me the way to   go past   go straight on
> junction   keep going   roundabout   take the first on the left
> take the second exit   take the second on the right   traffic lights
> turn left   turn left   turn right   turn right

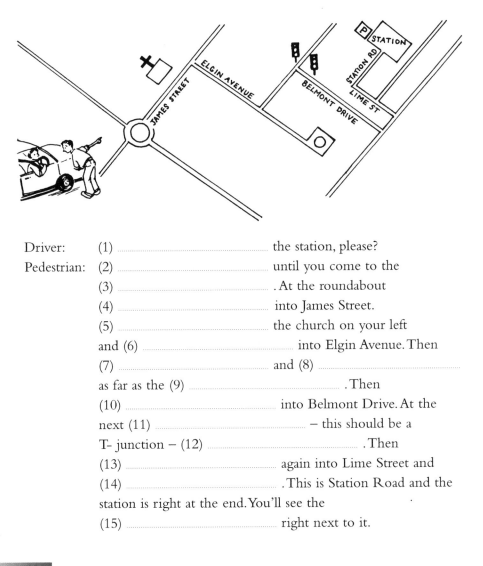

Driver:      (1) .................................... the station, please?

Pedestrian:  (2) .................................... until you come to the

(3) .................................... . At the roundabout

(4) .................................... into James Street.

(5) .................................... the church on your left

and (6) .................................... into Elgin Avenue. Then

(7) .................................... and (8) ....................................

as far as the (9) .................................... . Then

(10) .................................... into Belmont Drive. At the

next (11) .................................... – this should be a

T- junction – (12) .................................... . Then

(13) .................................... again into Lime Street and

(14) .................................... . This is Station Road and the

station is right at the end. You'll see the

(15) .................................... right next to it.

# 40 On the phone

**A** **Complete the sentences with the words in the box. Remember to put the verbs in the correct form.**

> answer  calling  engaged  hang up  Hello  machine
> message  mobile  pick  public  speak  wrong

I was out shopping when I remembered I was supposed to call my friend about going out that evening. I looked everywhere for a
(1) .......................... phone, but couldn't find one anywhere. Then I
remembered I had my (2) .......................... phone in my bag.
The first few times I called it was (3) .......................... . I thought she was
probably talking to her boyfriend. They're always calling each other.
The next time I tried there was no (4) .......................... , so I left a
(5) .......................... on the answering (6) .......................... , telling
her to call me. I waited and waited, but she didn't call, so I tried again.
Finally someone (7) .......................... up the phone and said
'(8) .......................... ?'
   'Could I (9) .......................... to Donna, please?' I asked.
   'Who's (10) .......................... , please?' the person asked.
   'It's Tina,' I said.
   Then to my surprise, he just said, 'Sorry, I think you've got the
(11) .......................... number.' And then he just (12) .......................... .

# Test 4 (Units 31–40)

**A** Write the opposites of these adjectives.

1 bent ...........................     4 dry ...........................

2 dark ...........................     5 heavy ...........................

3 smooth ...........................     6 sharp ...........................

**B** Complete the sentences with *do* or *make* or another verb that has an irregular past tense. Remember to put the verbs in the correct form.

I've had a terrible day. I got up at six o'clock, (1) ........................... the bed, had a shower, (2) ........................... my teeth and went downstairs. I (3) ........................... the dishes from yesterday and (4) ........................... myself a nice cup of tea. But then I dropped the milk jug and it (5) ........................... into pieces. I cleaned it up and decided to (6) ........................... the shopping. I (7) ........................... to take my wallet, so I had to walk all the way home again. It was twelve o'clock by this time, so I (8) ........................... lunch. After lunch I (9) ........................... a few phone calls and decided to go out again. Even before I got to the shops a big dog ran at me and (10) ........................... me on the leg. Now I'm at the hospital waiting to see a doctor.

**C** The <u>underlined</u> words are in the wrong sentences. Write the correct word for each sentence.

1 If you are frightened, you <u>clap</u>. ...........................

2 If you are saying hello or goodbye to someone, you <u>scream</u>. ...........................

3 If you want to show someone where something is, you <u>cry</u>. ...........................

4 If you think someone's performance is very good, you <u>whisper</u>. ...........................

5 If you think something is funny, you <u>wave</u>. ...........................

6 If you don't want someone to hear what you are saying, you <u>knock</u>. ...........................

7 If you are sad, you <u>laugh</u>. ...........................

8 If you want to enter someone's room, you <u>point</u>. ...........................

**D** Write the correct words to complete the phrasal verbs.

1 fill .............................. this form    fill .............................. your glass
2 take .............................. your father    take .............................. a company
3 get .............................. your colleagues    get .............................. the flu

**E** Join the sentences on the left with the replies on the right.

1 (Here, have a chocolate.)          (You're welcome.)
2 (Sorry, I can't go tonight.)          (Oh, sorry.)
3 (Thank you so much.)          (It doesn't matter.)
4 (You've spilt your drink on my coat.)          (Thank you.)

**F** Write the directions for each picture.

1

2

.................................................    .................................................
.................................................    .................................................

3

4

.................................................    .................................................
.................................................    .................................................

**G** Complete the sentences.

1 If you ring and I'm not in, .............................. on the answering machine.
2 Who were you talking to? I rang, but it was .............................. .
3 Please don't .............................. . I need to talk to you.
4 I rang, but there was .............................. . No one was in.
5 Is that 8893 1597? No? Oh sorry, I've got the .............................. .

# Answer Key

## 1 The family

**A**
1 *son-in-law*
2 step-father
3 grandparents
4 daughter-in-law
5 step-son
6 step-daughter
7 mother-in-law
8 brother-in-law
9 step-mother
10 great-grandmother
11 great-grandfather
12 father-in-law
13 sister-in-law
14 step-sister
15 step-brother

## 2 People you know

**A**
**family**
relative
**school**
classmate
**where you live**
neighbour
**love**
boyfriend
girlfriend

**work**
boss
colleague
**other**
*acquaintance*
close friend
friend of the family
mate

**B**
1 *mates*
2 an acquaintance
3 boss
4 colleagues
5 classmates
6 neighbours
7 relatives
8 boyfriend
9 friend of the family
10 girlfriend
11 a close friend

## 3 Clothes

**A**
**beach holiday**
bikini
sandals
sunglasses
sunhat
swimming costume
trunks

**walking holiday**
fleece
walking boots
waterproof jacket

**B**
1 sandals
2 bikini
3 swimming costume
4 walking boots
5 sunhat
6 trunks
7 waterproof jacket
8 fleece
9 sunglasses

**C**
1 *slippers*
2 dressing gown
3 knickers
4 nightie
5 underpants
6 bra
7 pyjamas
8 vest

## 4 Clothes and accessories

**A**
1 *lipstick*
2 earrings
3 comb
4 wallet
5 bracelet
6 shoelaces
7 ring
8 belt
9 purse
10 necklace

## 5 Life

**A**
1 was born
2 moved house
3 grew up
4 started school
5 went to university
6 fell in love
7 got engaged
8 got married
9 had a baby
10 retired
11 got divorced
12 died

## 6 Describing character

**A**

| bad qualities | good qualities |
|---|---|
| impatient | generous |
| mean | lovely |
| rude | patient |
| selfish | polite |
| silly | sensible |

**B**
1 j
2 a
3 d
4 f
5 b
6 e
7 c
8 i
9 h
10 g

## 7 Describing appearance

**A**
1 cute
2 dark-skinned
3 elegant
4 fair-skinned
5 good-looking
6 overweight
7 plain
8 pretty
9 scruffy
10 slim
11 smart
12 trendy

**B**
1 good-looking
2 smart
3 overweight
4 fair-skinned
5 cute
6 plain
7 dark-skinned
8 trendy
9 scruffy
10 pretty
11 slim
12 elegant

## 8 How you feel

**A**
1 *cheerful*
2 relaxed
3 pleased
4 annoyed
5 proud
6 fed up

**B**
1 *miserable*
2 jealous
3 guilty
4 surprised
5 worried
6 embarrassed

## 9 Having a bad day

**A**
1 h
2 c
3 j
4 f
5 a
6 d
7 e
8 i
9 b
10 g

**B**
1 *overslept*
2 missed
3 was late
4 fell over
5 got lost
6 were stuck in a traffic jam
7 ran out of
8 broke down
9 spilt
10 had an argument

## 10 Accidents and injuries

**A**
1 *swollen*; d
2 burn; c
3 broken; b
4 cut; f
5 black; a
6 bruise; e

**B**
1 had an accident
2 unconscious
3 injured
4 bleeding
5 pain
6 treatment
7 stitches
8 hurt
9 bandage

# Test 1 (Units 1–10)

**A**
1 brother-in-law
2 colleague
3 neighbour
4 mother-in-law
5 step-mother
6 great-grandfather
7 boss
8 step-son

**B** Gemma
**appearance**
overweight
plain
scruffy
**clothes and accessories**
dressing gown
pyjamas
slippers
Sarah
**appearance**
pretty
slim
smart
**clothes and accessories**
bikini
bracelet
earrings
necklace
sandals
sunglasses
sunhat

**C**
1 be born
2 start school
3 fall in love
4 get engaged
5 get married
6 have a baby
7 retire
8 die

**D**
1 generous
2 selfish
3 silly
4 impatient
5 rude
6 sensible

**E**
1 miserable, had an argument
2 embarrassed, fell over
3 annoyed, spilt
4 guilty, had an accident
5 worried, is late
6 pleased, isn't in pain

**F**
1 stitches
2 burn
3 bandage
4 swollen
5 unconscious
6 bruise

## 11 Shops and shopping

**A**
1 supermarket
2 department store
3 chemist's
4 newsagent's
5 hairdresser's
6 trolley
7 clothes shop
8 butcher's
9 baker's
10 basket
11 gift shop
12 checkout

**B**
1 shop assistant
2 try on
3 fit
4 changing room
5 cost
6 till
7 pay
8 receipt

## 12 Houses and homes

**A**
1 *I live in a house.*
2 I live in a bungalow.
3 I live in a cottage.
4 I live in a flat.

**B**
1 detached
2 block of
3 semi-detached
4 terraced

**C**
1 ground floor
2 second floor
3 first floor
4 basement

## 13 Housework

**A**
1 duster
2 vacuum cleaner
3 washing machine
4 dustbin
5 washing line
6 pegs
7 dishwasher
8 iron
9 ironing board

**B**
**do the dishes**
dishwasher
**do the ironing**
iron
ironing board
**do the washing**
pegs
washing line
washing machine

**dust**
duster
**hoover**
vacuum cleaner
**put the rubbish out**
dustbin

## 14 In the kitchen

**A**
1 pan
2 corkscrew
3 tap
4 mug
5 tin opener
6 tea towel
7 frying pan
8 bottle opener
9 food processor
10 coffee maker
11 washing-up liquid
12 teapot

**B**
**for cleaning**
tap
tea towel
washing-up liquid
**for opening things**
bottle opener
corkscrew
tin opener

**for drinks**
coffee maker
mug
teapot
**for cooking**
food processor
frying pan
pan

## 15 Food

**A**
*bread rolls*
cereal
cucumber
eggs
frozen vegetables
melon
pineapple
tinned fruit

**B**
1 sausages
2 bacon
3 cheese
4 red pepper
5 aubergine
6 dried fruit

## 16 Health and fitness

**A**
1 *healthy*
2 fit
3 lose weight
4 be good for you
5 exercise
6 keep fit
7 be bad for you
8 unfit
9 healthy diet
10 put on weight
11 unhealthy

**B**
1 *fit*
2 healthy
3 lose weight
4 put on weight
5 bad for you
6 unhealthy
7 good for you
8 healthy diet
9 exercise
10 keep fit
11 unfit

## 17 Sport

**A**
1 pitch
2 court
3 track

**B**
1 match
2 player
3 score
4 goal
5 team
6 win
7 lose
8 game
9 scored
10 point
11 win
12 player
13 win
14 race

## 18 Music

**A** **types of music**
classical music
jazz
opera
pop music

**people**
band
choir
composer
conductor
orchestra
pop star
singer

**B** 1 I like jazz.
2 I like opera.
3 I like pop music.
4 I like classical music.

**C** 1 singer
2 conductor
3 orchestra
4 choir
5 composer
6 band
7 pop star

## 19 Shapes

**A** 1 *star*
2 circle
3 rectangle
4 squares
5 circle
6 hearts
7 oval
8 diamonds
9 rectangle
10 triangles
11 triangle
12 circles

**B** 1 square, square, rectangular, triangular
2 star-shaped, circular
3 heart-shaped
4 oval, triangular
5 diamond-shaped

## 20 Measurements

**A** **swimming pool**
1 length
2 width
3 depth

**man**
1 height
2 weight

**B** 1 long
2 heavy
3 wide
4 high
5 tall
6 deep
7 weigh

## Test 2 (Units 11–20)

**A** 1 newsagent's
2 chemist's
3 terraced
4 cottage

**B** 1 hoover
2 dishes
3 ironing
4 dust

**C** 1 tea towel
2 corkscrew
3 frying pan
4 bottle opener
5 teapot
6 tin opener

**D** 1 eggs
2 bacon
3 cheese
4 sausage

**E** 1 unfit
2 race
3 healthy
4 scored

**F** 1 jazz
2 orchestra
3 choir
4 composer

**G**

**H** 1 length
2 heavy
3 width
4 tall

58

## 21 Jobs

**A**
1 a cleaner
2 a photographer
3 an accountant
4 a civil servant
5 a computer programmer

**B**
1 *Eric*, Tim, Michelle
2 Janice, Lena

**C**
1 journalist
2 model
3 au pair
4 shop assistant

## 22 In the office

**A**
1 filing cabinet
2 file
3 desk tidy
4 Post-it™ note
5 notepad
6 diary
7 ring binder
8 calculator
9 stapler
10 paper clip
11 hole punch
12 in-tray/out-tray

**B**
1 paper clip
2 stapler
3 desk tidy
4 Post-it™ note
5 notepad
6 diary

## 23 Writing to people

**A**
1 a memo
2 a letter
3 a postcard
4 an email
5 a note
6 a fax
7 a text message

**B**
1 writing paper
2 postcode
3 address
4 stamp
5 envelope

## 24 Holidays

**A**
1 camping holiday
2 beach holiday
3 walking holiday
4 skiing holiday
5 cruise

**B**
1 hotels
2 youth hostel
3 villas
4 bed and breakfast
5 tent

**C**
1 d
2 a
3 b
4 c

## 25 Hotels

**A**
1 c
2 e
3 b
4 h
5 j
6 i
7 l
8 a
9 g
10 k
11 d
12 f

**B**
1 reservation
2 book
3 fully booked
4 twin room
5 ensuite

## 26 Travelling by plane

**A**
1 departures
2 check-in desk
3 passport control
4 departure lounge
5 gate
6 baggage reclaim
7 customs
8 arrivals

**B**
1 boarding card, flight
2 aboard
3 hand luggage, overhead locker
4 life jacket
5 take-off, landing

## 27 In the countryside

**A**
1 *footpath*
2 farm
3 fields
4 river
5 bridge
6 waterfall
7 forest
8 lake
9 mountains
10 valley
11 lane
12 village

## 28 The weather

**A**
1 forecast
2 sunshine
3 south
4 showers
5 west
6 icy
7 hail
8 east
9 frost
10 east
11 thunder and lightning
12 north
13 mild
14 south

## 29 Animals

**A**
**animals with wings**
butterfly
fly
owl
**animals that live in water**
crab
frog
octopus
shark
whale

**other**
bear
deer
fox
kangaroo
rat
spider

**B**
1 bear
2 rat
3 frog
4 whale
5 fly
6 deer
7 fox

**C**
1 owl
2 kangaroo
3 spider
4 crab
5 octopus
6 shark
7 butterfly

## 30 Parts of a car

**A**
1 boot
2 windscreen
3 wing mirror
4 engine
5 headlight
6 tyre
7 seatbelt
8 windscreen wipers
9 wheel
10 indicator
11 bumper

**B**
1 headlights
2 tyres
3 boot
4 indicator
5 seatbelt
6 windscreen wipers

## Test 3 (Units 21–30)

**A**
1 journalist
2 civil servant
3 shop assistant
4 accountant

**B**
1 paper clip
2 calculator
3 desk tidy
4 filing cabinet

**C**
1 mountains
2 lake
3 river
4 waterfall
5 bridge

**D**
1 fax
2 email
3 text message
4 letter

**E**
1 beach holiday
2 booked
3 single
4 flight
5 departure lounge
6 guidebook
7 hand luggage
8 take-off

**F**
1 showers
2 frost
3 sunshine
4 thunder and lightning

**G animals that can fly**
fly
butterfly
owl
**animals that can swim**
crab
shark
whale

**H**
1 windscreen
2 boot
3 seatbelt
4 engine

## 31 Everyday adjectives

**A**
1 *rough*
2 blunt
3 dark
4 light
5 bent
6 dry

**B**
1 heavy
2 light
3 dark
4 light
5 sharp
6 blunt
7 dry
8 wet
9 straight
10 bent
11 smooth
12 rough

## 32 Using your voice

**A**
1 whispered
2 speak
3 talking
4 sing
5 cry
6 announced
7 said

**B**
1 stutter
2 chat
3 shout
4 tell
5 laugh
6 scream
7 cheer

## 33 Using your hands

**A**
1 wave
2 clap
3 pick
4 tickle
5 point
6 stroke
7 pat
8 pinch
9 knock
10 scratch

**B**
1 *He's waving to his friend.*
2 They're clapping because they enjoyed the show.
3 She's picking a flower.
4 She's tickling the little boy.
5 He's pointing to a word.
6 She's stroking the cat.
7 They're patting the dog's head.
8 He's pinching her arm.
9 She's knocking on the door.
10 He's scratching his head.

## 34 Do and make

**A**

| do | make |
|---|---|
| *business* | a cake |
| exercise | friends |
| your | a mistake |
| homework | money |
| the housework | a noise |
| your teeth | |

**B**
1. *make a speech*
2. make the bed
3. do the shopping
4. make a phone call
5. do an exam
6. make a cup of tea
7. make an appointment
8. do your hair
9. do the dishes
10. make lunch

## 35 Irregular past tenses

**A**

| | | | |
|---|---|---|---|
| 1 *bit* | 8 kept | | |
| 2 blew | 9 lost | | |
| 3 broke | 10 put | | |
| 4 drew | 11 rode | | |
| 5 found | 12 smelt | | |
| 6 forgot | 13 taught | | |
| 7 grew | 14 threw | | |

**B**

| | | | |
|---|---|---|---|
| 1 smelt | 8 found | | |
| 2 threw | 9 forgot | | |
| 3 lost | 10 kept | | |
| 4 rode | 11 drew | | |
| 5 put | 12 broke | | |
| 6 bit | 13 taught | | |
| 7 blew | 14 grew | | |

## 36 Phrasal verbs with *off* and *up*

**A**

| | |
|---|---|
| 1 up | 6 up |
| 2 off | 7 up |
| 3 off | 8 off |
| 4 up | 9 off |
| 5 off | 10 up |

**B**
1. *grow up*
2. take off
3. put off
4. save up
5. tell off
6. show off

**C**
1. *bring up*
2. hurry up
3. give up
4. go off

## 37 More phrasal verbs

**A**

| | |
|---|---|
| 1 *run* | 6 taken |
| 2 get | 7 looks |
| 3 fill | 8 run |
| 4 Look | 9 filling |
| 5 get | 10 take |

**B**
1. fill up
2. run out
3. run away
4. look out

**C**
1. look after
2. take after
3. fill in
4. get on with
5. get over
6. take over

## 38 Sorry and thank you

**A**
1. *OK*
2. problem
3. matter
4. mention
5. apologise
6. thank
7. mind
8. sorry
9. worry
10. thanks
11. welcome

## 39 Giving directions

**A** 1 Could you tell me the way to
2 Go straight on
3 roundabout
4 take the second exit
5 Go past
6 turn right
7 take the first on the left
8 keep going
9 traffic lights
10 turn right
11 junction
12 turn left
13 turn left
14 take the second on the right
15 car park

## 40 On the phone

**A** 1 public
2 mobile
3 engaged
4 answer
5 message
6 machine
7 picked
8 Hello
9 speak
10 calling
11 wrong
12 hung up

## Test 4 (Units 31–40)

**A** 1 straight
2 light
3 rough
4 wet
5 light
6 blunt

**B** 1 made
2 did
3 did
4 made
5 broke
6 do
7 forgot
8 made
9 made
10 bit

**C** 1 scream
2 wave
3 point
4 clap
5 laugh
6 whisper
7 cry
8 knock

**D** 1 in, up
2 after, over
3 on with, over

**E** 1 Thank you.
2 It doesn't matter.
3 You're welcome.
4 Oh, sorry.

**F** 1 turn left
2 take the second on the right
3 go past
4 take the second exit

**G** 1 leave a message
2 engaged
3 hang up
4 no answer
5 wrong number

# Word List

The words in this list are British English. Sometimes we give you an important American English word which means the same.

## 1 The family

brother-in-law /'brʌðərɪnlɔː/
daughter-in-law /'dɔːtərɪnlɔː/
father-in-law /'fɑːðərɪnlɔː/
grandparents /'græn,peərənts/
great-grandfather /,greɪt'græn,fɑːðə/
great-grandmother /,greɪt'græn,mʌðə/
mother-in-law /'mʌðərɪnlɔː/
sister-in-law /'sɪstərɪnlɔː/
son-in-law /'sʌnɪnlɔː/
step-brother /'stepbrʌðə/
step-daughter /'stepdɔːtə/
step-father /'stepfɑːðə/
step-mother /'stepmʌðə/
step-sister /'stepsɪstə/
step-son /'stepsʌn/

## 2 People you know

acquaintance /ə'kweɪntəns/
boss /bɒs/
boyfriend /'bɔɪfrend/
classmate /'klɑːsmeɪt/
close friend /,kləʊs 'frend/
colleague /'kɒliːg/
friend of the family /,frend əv ðə 'fæməli/
girlfriend /'gɜːlfrend/
mate /meɪt/ (informal)
neighbour /'neɪbə/
relative /'relətɪv/

## 3 Clothes

bikini /bɪˈkiːni/
bra /brɑː/
dressing gown /ˈdresɪŋ gaʊn/ (US = robe)
fleece /fliːs/
knickers /ˈnɪkəz/ (Use with a plural verb, e.g. My knickers *are* white. Or a pair of knickers. US = panties)
nightie /ˈnaɪti/
pyjamas /pɪˈdʒɑːməz/ (US = pajamas)
sandals /ˈsændəlz/
slippers /ˈslɪpəz/
sunglasses /ˈsʌnˌglɑːsɪz/
sunhat /ˈsʌn hæt/
swimming costume /ˈswɪmɪŋ ˌkɒstjuːm/ (US = bathing suit)
trunks /trʌŋks/ (Use with a plural verb, e.g. My trunks *are* green.)
underpants /ˈʌndəpænts/ (Use with a plural verb, e.g. My underpants *are* white. Or a pair of underpants)
vest /vest/ (US = undershirt)
walking boots /ˈwɔːkɪŋ buːts/
waterproof jacket /ˌwɔːtəpruːf ˈdʒækɪt/

## 4 Clothes and accessories

belt /belt/
bracelet /ˈbreɪslət/
comb /kəʊm/
earrings /ˈɪərɪŋz/
lipstick /ˈlɪpstɪk/
necklace /ˈnekləs/
purse /pɜːs/ (in US English this word means handbag)
ring /rɪŋ/
shoelaces /ˈʃuːleɪsɪz/
wallet /ˈwɒlɪt/

## 5 Life

be born /biː ˈbɔːn/ (*past tense* was/were; *past participle* been)
die /daɪ/
fall in love /ˌfɔːl ɪn ˈlʌv/ (*past tense* fell; *past participle* fallen)
get divorced /ˌget dɪˈvɔːst/ (*past tense & past participle* got)

get engaged /ˌget ɪnˈgeɪdʒd/ (*past tense & past participle* got)
get married /ˌget ˈmærɪd/ (*past tense & past participle* got)
go to university /ˌgəʊ tə ˌjuːnɪˈvɜːsəti/ (*past tense* went; *past participle* gone)
grow up /ˌgrəʊ ˈʌp/ (*past tense* grew; *past participle* grown)
have a baby /ˌhæv ə ˈbeɪbi/ (*past tense & past participle* had)
move house /ˌmuːv ˈhaʊs/
start school /ˌstɑːt ˈskuːl/
retire /rɪˈtaɪə/

## 6 Describing character

generous /ˈdʒenərəs/
impatient /ɪmˈpeɪʃənt/
lovely /ˈlʌvli/
mean /miːn/
patient /ˈpeɪʃənt/
polite /pəˈlaɪt/
rude /ruːd/
selfish /ˈselfɪʃ/
sensible /ˈsensɪbl/
silly /ˈsɪli/

## 7 Describing appearance

cute /kjuːt/ (usually used about a child or baby. In US English also used about men and women)
dark-skinned /ˌdɑːkˈskɪnd/
elegant /ˈelɪgənt/ (used about a woman)
fair-skinned /ˌfeəˈskɪnd/
good-looking /ˌgʊdˈlʊkɪŋ/
overweight /ˌəʊvəˈweɪt/
plain /pleɪn/ (polite for *ugly*, usually used about a woman)
pretty /ˈprɪti/ (used about a woman)
scruffy /ˈskrʌfi/
slim /slɪm/ (an approving word)
smart /smɑːt/
trendy /ˈtrendi/ (an informal word)

## 8 How you feel

annoyed /ə'nɔɪd/
cheerful /'tʃɪəfəl/
embarrassed /ɪmˈbærəst/
fed up /ˌfed 'ʌp/ (informal)
guilty /'ɡɪlti/
jealous /'dʒeləs/
miserable /'mɪzrəbl/
pleased /pliːzd/
proud /praʊd/
relaxed /rɪˈlækst/
surprised /səˈpraɪzd/
worried /'wʌrid/

## 9 Having a bad day

be late /biː 'leɪt/ (past tense was/were; past participle been)
be stuck in a traffic jam /biː ˌstʌk ɪn ə 'træfɪk ˌdʒæm/
break down /ˌbreɪk 'daʊn/ (past tense broke; past participle broken)
fall over /ˌfɔːl 'əʊvə/ (past tense fell; past participle fallen)
get lost /ˌget 'lɒst/ (past tense & past participle got)
have an argument /ˌhæv ən 'ɑːgjəmənt/ (past tense & past participle had)
miss /mɪs/
oversleep /ˌəʊvə'sliːp/ (past tense & past participle overslept)
run out of /ˌrʌn 'aʊt əv/ (past tense ran; past participle run)
spill /spɪl/ (past tense & past participle spilled UK also spilt)

## 10 Accidents and injuries

bandage /'bændɪdʒ/
be in pain /biː ɪn 'peɪn/
black eye /ˌblæk 'aɪ/
bleed /bliːd/ (past tense & past participle bled)
broken /'brəʊkən/
bruise /bruːz/
burn /bɜːn/
cut /kʌt/
have an accident /hæv ən 'æksɪdənt/
hurt /hɜːt/ (past tense & past participle hurt)
injured /'ɪndʒəd/

Word List

stitches /ˈstɪtʃɪz/
swollen /ˈswəʊlən/
treatment /ˈtriːtmənt/
unconscious /ʌnˈkɒnʃəs/

## 11 Shops and shopping

baker's /ˈbeɪkəz/
basket /ˈbɑːskɪt/
butcher's /ˈbʊtʃəz/
changing room /ˈtʃeɪndʒɪŋ ˌruːm/
checkout /ˈtʃekaʊt/
chemist's /ˈkemɪsts/
clothes shop /ˈkləʊðz ʃɒp/
cost /kɒst/ (*past tense & past participle* cost)
department store /dɪˈpɑːtmənt ˌstɔː/
fit /fɪt/
gift shop /ˈgɪft ʃɒp/
hairdresser's /ˈheədresəz/
newsagent's /ˈnjuːzˌeɪdʒənts/
pay by cheque / credit card /ˌpeɪ ˈbaɪ tʃek / ˈkredɪt ˌkɑːd/
receipt /rɪˈsiːt/
shop assistant /ˈʃɒp əsɪstənt/
supermarket /ˈsuːpəˌmɑːkɪt/
till /tɪl/
trolley /ˈtrɒli/
try on /ˌtraɪ ˈɒn/

## 12 Houses and homes

basement /ˈbeɪsmənt/
block of flats /ˈblɒk əv flæts/
bungalow /ˈbʌŋgələʊ/
cottage /ˈkɒtɪdʒ/
detached /dɪˈtætʃt/
first floor /ˌfɜːst ˈflɔː/ (in US English this means ground floor)
flat /flæt/
ground floor /ˌgraʊnd ˈflɔː/
house /haʊs/
second floor /ˌsekənd ˈflɔː/ (in US English this means first floor)
semi-detached /ˌsemidɪˈtætʃt/
terraced /ˈterɪst/

## 13 Housework

dishwasher /'dɪʃˌwɒʃə/
do the dishes /ˌduː ðə 'dɪʃɪz/
do the ironing /ˌduː ðɪ 'aɪənɪŋ/
do the washing /ˌduː ðə 'wɒʃɪŋ/
dust /dʌst/
dustbin /'dʌsbɪn/
duster /'dʌstə/
hoover /'huːvə/
iron /'aɪən/
ironing board /'aɪənɪŋ ˌbɔːd/
pegs /pegz/
put the rubbish out /ˌpʊt ðə 'rʌbɪʃ aʊt/
vacuum cleaner /'vækjuːm ˌkliːnə/
washing line /'wɒʃɪŋ ˌlaɪn/
washing machine /'wɒʃɪŋ məˌʃiːn/

## 14 In the kitchen

bottle opener /'bɒtl ˌəʊpənə/
coffee maker /'kɒfi meɪkə/
corkscrew /'kɔːkskruː/
food processor /'fuːd prəʊsesə/
frying pan /'fraɪɪŋ pæn/
mug /mʌg/
pan /pæn/
tap /tæp/
teapot /'tiːpɒt/
tea towel /'tiː ˌtaʊəl/
tin opener /'tɪn əʊpənə/
washing-up liquid /ˌwɒʃɪŋ'ʌp ˌlɪkwɪd/

## 15 Food

aubergine /'əʊbəʒiːn/ (US = eggplant)
bacon /'beɪkən/
bread rolls /ˌbred 'rəʊlz/
cereal /'sɪəriəl/
cheese /tʃiːz/
cucumber /'kjuːkʌmbə/

dried fruit /ˌdraɪd 'fruːt/
eggs /egz/
frozen vegetables /ˌfrəʊzən 'vedʒtəblz/
melon /'melən/
red pepper /ˌred pepə/
pineapple /'paɪnæpl/
sausages /'sɒsɪdʒɪz/
tinned fruit /ˌtɪnd 'fruːt/

## 16 Health and fitness

be bad for you /biː 'bæd fə juː/
be good for you /biː 'gʊd fə juː/
exercise /'eksəsaɪz/
fit /fɪt/
healthy /'helθi/
healthy diet /ˌhelθi 'daɪət/
keep fit /ˌkiːp fɪt/
lose weight /ˌluːz 'weɪt/
put on weight /ˌpʊt ɒn 'weɪt/
unfit /ʌn'fɪt/
unhealthy /ʌn'helθi/

## 17 Sport

court /kɔːt/
game /geɪm/
goal /gəʊl/
lose /luːz/ (*past tense & past participle* lost)
match /mætʃ/
pitch /pɪtʃ/
player /pleɪə/
point /pɔɪnt/
race /reɪs/
score /skɔː/
team /tiːm/
track /træk/
win /wɪn/ (*past tense & past participle* won)

## 18 Music

band /bænd/
choir /kwaɪə/
classical music /ˌklæsɪkəl ˈmjuːzɪk/
composer /kəmˈpəʊzə/
conductor /kənˈdʌktə/
jazz /dʒæz/
opera /ˈɒpərə/
orchestra /ˈɔːkɪstrə/
pop music /ˈpɒp ˌmjuːzɪk/
pop star /ˈpɒp ˌstɑː/
singer /ˈsɪŋə/

## 19 Shapes

circle /ˈsɜːkl/
circular /ˈsɜːkjələ/
diamond /ˈdaɪəmənd/
diamond-shaped /ˈdaɪəməndʃeɪpt/
heart /hɑːt/
heart-shaped /ˈhɑːtʃeɪpt/
oval /ˈəʊvəl/ (noun and adjective)
rectangle /ˈrektæŋgl/
rectangular /rekˈtæŋgjələ/
square /skweə/ (noun and adjective)
star /stɑː/
star-shaped /ˈstɑːʃeɪpt/
triangle /ˈtraɪæŋgl/
triangular /traɪˈæŋgjələ/

## 20 Measurements

deep /diːp/
depth /depθ/
heavy /ˈhevi/
height /haɪt/
high /haɪ/
length /leŋθ/
long /lɒŋ/

tall /tɔːl/ (how tall are you?)
weigh /weɪ/ (how much do you weigh?)
weight /weɪt/
wide /waɪd/
width /wɪtθ/

## 21 Jobs

accountant /əˈkaʊntənt/
au pair /ˌəʊˈpeə/
civil servant /ˌsɪvəl ˈsɜːvənt/
cleaner /ˈkliːnə/
computer programmer /kəmpjuːtə ˈprəʊgræmə/
full-time /ˌfʊlˈtaɪm/
journalist /ˈdʒɜːnəlɪst/
model /ˈmɒdəl/
part-time /ˌpɑːtˈtaɪm/
photographer /fəˈtɒgrəfə/
shop assistant /ˈʃɒp əsɪstənt/

## 22 In the office

calculator /ˈkælkjəleɪtə/
desk tidy /ˈdesk taɪdi/
diary /ˈdaɪəri/
file /faɪl/
filing cabinet /ˈfaɪlɪŋ ˌkæbɪnət/
hole punch /ˈhəʊl ˌpʌnʃ/
in-tray/out-tray /ˈɪntreɪ / ˈaʊttreɪ/
notepad /ˈnəʊtpæd/
paper clip /ˈpeɪpə klɪp/
Post-it™ note /ˈpəʊstɪt ˌnəʊt/
ring binder /ˈrɪŋ baɪndə/
stapler /ˈsteɪplə/

## 23 Writing to people
address /əˈdres/
email /ˈiːmeɪl/
envelope /ˈenvələʊp/
fax /fæks/
letter /ˈletə/
memo /ˈmeməʊ/
note /nəʊt/
postcard /ˈpəʊskɑːd/
postcode /ˈpəʊskəʊd/
stamp /stæmp/
text message /ˈtekst ˌmesɪdʒ/
writing paper /ˈraɪtɪŋ ˌpeɪpə/

## 24 Holidays
beach holiday /ˈbiːtʃ ˌhɒlədeɪ/
bed and breakfast /bed ən ˈbrekfəst/
camping holiday /ˈkæmpɪŋ ˌhɒlədeɪ/
cruise /kruːz/
foreign currency /ˌfɒrɪn ˈkʌrənsi/
guidebook /ˈgaɪdbʊk/
hotel /həʊˈtel/
skiing holiday /ˈskiːɪŋ ˌhɒlədeɪ/
tent /tent/
vaccination /ˌvæksɪˈneɪʃən/
villa /ˈvɪlə/
visa /ˈviːzə/
walking holiday /ˈwɔːkɪŋ ˌhɒlədeɪ/
youth hostel /ˈjuːθ ˌhɒstəl/

## 25 Hotels
book /bʊk/
double room /ˌdʌbl ˈruːm/
ensuite /ˌɒn ˈswiːt/
full board /ˌfʊl ˈbɔːd/
fully booked /ˌfʊli ˈbʊkt/
half board /ˌhɑːf ˈbɔːd/
reception /rɪˈsepʃən/

receptionist /rɪˈsepʃənɪst/
reservation /ˌrezəˈveɪʃən/
room service /ˈruːm ˌsɜːvɪs/
single room /ˌsɪŋgl ˈruːm/
twin room /ˈtwɪn ˌruːm/

## 26 Travelling by plane

aboard /əˈbɔːd/
arrivals /əˈraɪvəlz/
baggage reclaim /ˈbægɪdʒ ˌrɪkleɪm/
boarding card /ˈbɔːdɪŋ ˌkɑːd/
check-in desk /ˈtʃekɪn ˌdesk/
customs /ˈkʌstəmz/
departure lounge /dɪˈpɑːtʃə ˌlaʊndʒ/
departures /dɪˈpɑːtʃəz/
flight /flaɪt/
gate /geɪt/
hand luggage /ˈhænd ˌlʌgɪdʒ/
landing /ˈlændɪŋ/
life jacket /ˈlaɪf ˌdʒækɪt/
overhead locker /ˌəʊvəhed ˈlɒkə/
passport control /ˈpɑːspɔːt ˌkəntrəʊl/
take-off /ˈteɪkɒf/

## 27 In the countryside

bridge /brɪdʒ/
farm /fɑːm/
fields /ˈfiːldz/
footpath /ˈfʊtpɑːθ/
forest /ˈfɒrɪst/
lake /leɪk/
lane /leɪn/
mountains /ˈmaʊntɪnz/
river /ˈrɪvə/
valley /ˈvæli/
village /ˈvɪlɪdʒ/
waterfall /ˈwɔːtəfɔːl/

## 28 The weather

east /iːst/
forecast /ˈfɔːkɑːst/
frost /frɒst/
hail /heɪl/
icy /ˈaɪsi/
lightning /ˈlaɪtnɪŋ/
mild /maɪld/
north /nɔːθ/
showers /ˈʃaʊəz/
south /saʊθ/
sunshine /ˈsʌnʃaɪn/
thunder /ˈθʌndə/
west /west/

## 29 Animals

bear /beə/
butterfly /ˈbʌtəflaɪ/
crab /kræb/
deer /dɪə/ (plural = deer)
fly /flaɪ/
fox /fɒks/
frog /frɒg/
kangaroo /ˌkæŋgərˈuː/
octopus /ˈɒktəpəs/
owl /aʊl/
rat /ræt/
shark /ʃɑːk/
spider /ˈspaɪdə/
whale /weɪl/

## 30 Parts of a car

boot /buːt/ (US = trunk)
bumper /ˈbʌmpə/
engine /ˈendʒɪn/
headlight /ˈhedlaɪt/
indicator /ˈɪndɪkeɪtə/
seatbelt /ˈsiːtˌbelt/

tyre /taɪə/
wheel /wiːl/
windscreen /'wɪnskriːn/
windscreen wipers /'wɪnskriːn ˌwaɪpəz/
wing mirror /'wɪŋ ˌmɪrə/

## 31 Everyday adjectives

bent /bent/
blunt /blʌnt/
dark /dɑːk/
dry /draɪ/
heavy /'hevi/
light /laɪt/
rough /rʌf/
sharp /ʃɑːp/
smooth /smuːð/
straight /streɪt/
wet /wet/

## 32 Using your voice

announce /ə'naʊns/
chat /tʃæt/
cheer /tʃɪə/
cry /kraɪ/
laugh /lɑːf/
say /seɪ/ (*past tense & past participle* said)
scream /skriːm/
shout /ʃaʊt/
sing /sɪŋ/ (*past tense* sang; *past participle* sung)
speak /spiːk/ (*past tense* spoke; *past participle* spoken)
stutter /'stʌtə/
talk /tɔːk/
tell /tel/ (*past tense & past participle* told)
whisper /'wɪspə/

## 33 Using your hands

clap /klæp/
knock /nɒk/
pat /pæt/
pick /pɪk/
pinch /pɪnʃ/
point /pɔɪnt/
scratch /skrætʃ/
stroke /strəʊk/
tickle /'tɪkl/
wave /weɪv/

## 34 *Do* and *make*

do business /ˌduː 'bɪznɪs/
do the dishes /ˌduː ðə 'dɪʃɪz/
do an exam /ˌduː ən ɪg'zæm/
do exercise /ˌduː 'eksəsaɪz/
do your hair /ˌduː jə heə/
do your homework /ˌduː jə 'həʊmwɜːk/
do the housework /ˌduː ðə 'haʊswɜːk/
do the shopping /ˌduː ðə 'ʃɒpɪŋ/
do your teeth /ˌduː jə 'tiːθ/
make an appointment /ˌmeɪk ən ə'pɔɪntmənt/
make the bed /ˌmeɪk ðə bed/
make a cake /ˌmeɪk ə 'keɪk/
make a cup of tea /ˌmeɪk ə ˌkʌp əv 'tiː/
make friends /ˌmeɪk 'frendz/
make lunch /ˌmeɪk 'lʌnʃ/
make a mistake /ˌmeɪk ə mɪs'teɪk/
make money /ˌmeɪk 'mʌni/
make a noise /ˌmeɪk ə 'nɔɪz/
make a phone call /ˌmeɪk ə 'fəʊn kɔːl/
make a speech /ˌmeɪk ə 'spiːtʃ/

## 35 Irregular past tenses

bite /baɪt/ (*past tense* bit; *past participle* bitten)
blow /bləʊ/ (*past tense* blew; *past participle* blown)
break /breɪk/ (*past tense* broke; *past participle* broken)

draw /drɔː/ (*past tense* drew; *past participle* drawn)
find /faɪnd/ (*past tense* & *past participle* found)
forget /fə'get/ (*past tense* forgot; *past participle* forgotten)
grow /grəʊ/ (*past tense* grew; *past participle* grown)
keep /kiːp/ (*past tense* & *past participle* kept)
lose /luːz/ (*past tense* & *past participle* lost)
put /pʊt/ (*past tense* & *past participle* put)
ride /raɪd/ (*past tense* rode; *past participle* ridden)
smell /smel/ (*past tense* & *past participle* smelled *UK also* smelt)
teach /tiːtʃ/ (*past tense* & *past participle* taught)
throw /θrəʊ/ (*past tense* threw; *past participle* thrown)

## 36 Phrasal verbs with *off* and *up*

bring up /ˌbrɪŋ 'ʌp/ (*past tense* & *past participle* brought)
give up /ˌgɪv 'ʌp/ (*past tense* gave; *past participle* given)
go off /ˌgəʊ 'ɒf/ (*past tense* went; *past participle* gone)
grow up /ˌgrəʊ 'ʌp/ (*past tense* grew; *past participle* grown)
hurry up /ˌhʌri 'ʌp/
put off /ˌpʊt 'ɒf/ (*past tense* & *past participle* put)
save up /ˌseɪv 'ʌp/
show off /ˌʃəʊ 'ɒf/ (*past tense* showed; *past participle* shown)
take off /ˌteɪk 'ɒf/ (*past tense* took; *past participle* taken)
tell off /ˌtel 'ɒf/ (*past tense* & *past participle* told)

## 37 More phrasal verbs

fill in /ˌfɪl 'ɪn/
fill up /ˌfɪl 'ʌp/
get on with /ˌget 'ɒn wɪð/ (*past tense* got; *past participle* got *US also* gotten)
get over /ˌget 'əʊvə/ (*past tense* got; *past participle* got *US also* gotten)
look after /ˌlʊk 'ɑːftə/
look out! /ˌlʊk 'aʊt/
run away /ˌrʌn 'əweɪ/ (*past tense* ran; *past participle* run)
run out of /ˌrʌn 'aʊt əv/ (*past tense* ran; *past participle* run)
take after /ˌteɪk 'ɑːftə/ (*past tense* took; *past participle* taken)
take over /ˌteɪk 'əʊvə/ (*past tense* took; *past participle* taken)

## 38 Sorry and thank you

apologise /ə'pɒlədʒaɪz/
don't mention it /ˌdəʊnt 'menʃən ɪt/
don't worry /ˌdəʊnt 'wʌri/
it doesn't matter /ɪt ˌdʌzənt 'mætə/
never mind /ˌnevə 'maɪnd/
no problem /ˌnəʊ 'prɒbləm/
sorry /'sɒri/
thank you /'θæŋk juː/
thanks /θæŋks/ (informal)
that's OK /'ðæts ˌəʊkeɪ/
you're welcome /ˌjɔː 'welkəm/

## 39 Giving directions

car park /'kɑː ˌpɑːk/
could you tell me the way to /ˌkʊd juː ˌtel miː ðə 'weɪ tə/
go past /ˌgəʊ 'pɑːst/
go straight on /ˌgəʊ 'streɪt ˌɒn/
junction /'dʒʌŋkʃən/
keep going /ˌkiːp 'gəʊɪŋ/
roundabout /'raʊndəˌbaʊt/
take the first on the left /ˌteɪk ðə ˌfɜːst ɒn ðə 'left/
take the second exit /ˌteɪk ðə ˌsekənd 'eksɪt/
take the second on the right /ˌteɪk ðə ˌsekənd ɒn ðə 'raɪt/
traffic lights /'træfɪk ˌlaɪts/
turn left /ˌtɜːn 'left/
turn right /ˌtɜːn 'raɪt/

## 40 On the phone

answering machine /'ɑːnsərɪŋ məˌʃiːn/
Could I speak to … ? /'kʊd aɪ spiːk tə/
engaged /ɪn'geɪdʒd/
hang up /ˌhæŋ 'ʌp/
Hello /hel'əʊ/
leave a message /ˌliːv ə 'mesɪdʒ/
mobile phone /ˌməʊbaɪl 'fəʊn/
no answer /ˌnəʊ 'ɑːnsə/
pick up the phone /ˌpɪk ʌp ðə 'fəʊn/
public phone /ˌpʌblɪk 'fəʊn/
Who's calling, please? /ˌhuːz 'kɔːlɪŋ ˌpliːz/
wrong number /ˌrɒŋ 'nʌmbə/

# Acknowledgements

I am very grateful to all the schools, institutions, teachers and students around the world who either piloted or commented on the material:

Kristi Alcouffe, Alcouffe Formation, Paris, France
Graham Bathgate, Tokyo, Japan
Katie Head, Cambridge, UK
Magdalena Kijak, Krakow, Poland
Andrea Paul, Melbourne, Australia
Tadeusz Wolanski, Gdansk, Poland

I am also grateful to staff and students at the following institutions who tested the pilot material:

Transfer, Paris, France
IFG Langues, Paris, France
CEL Evry, Evry, France
Ibaraki University, Japan
Simul Academy, Shinjuku School, Tokyo, Japan

I would particularly like to thank Nóirín Burke and Martine Walsh at Cambridge University Press for all their help, guidance and support during the writing of this series. My thanks also to Liz Driscoll for her experienced editing of the material and to Jo Barker and Sarah Warburton for their excellent design and artwork.